Can I Retire?

How Much Money You Need to Retire and
How to Manage Your Retirement Savings,
Explained in 100 Pages or Less

Can I Retire?

How Much Money You Need to Retire and
How to Manage Your Retirement Savings,
Explained in 100 Pages or Less

Mike Piper

Simple Subjects, LLC
Chicago, Illinois 60626
ISBN: 978-0-9814542-5-2
www.ObliviousInvestor.com

Dedication

To every investor navigating his or her way through the morass of market uncertainty, tax complexity, and conflicting advice.

Why is there a lightbulb on the cover?

In cartoons and comics, a lightbulb is often used to signify a moment of clarity or sudden understanding—an "aha!" moment. My hope is that the books in the *"...in 100 pages or less"* series can help readers achieve clarity and understanding of topics that are often considered complex and confusing—hence the lightbulb.

Disclaimer

This text is intended to be an introduction to some of the most important topics relating to retirement planning. It is *not*, however, intended to be a substitute for personalized advice from a professional advisor. The author will make his best effort to keep the information current and accurate; however, given the ever-changing nature of the subject matter, no guarantee can be made as to the accuracy of the information contained within.

Your Feedback is Appreciated!

As the author of this book, I'm very interested to hear your thoughts. If you find the book helpful, please let me know! Alternatively, if you have any suggestions of ways to make the book better, I'm eager to hear that, too.

Finally, if you're unsatisfied with your purchase for any reason, let me know, and I'll be happy to provide you with a refund of the current list price of the book (limited to one refund per household).

You can reach me at: mike@simplesubjects.com.

Best Regards,
Mike Piper

Table of Contents

Introduction: Time to Make a Plan

Part One
How Much Money Will I Need to Retire?

Part Two
Retirement Portfolio Management

Part Three
Tax Planning in Retirement

INTRODUCTION

Time to Make a Plan

There are already several excellent books about retirement planning. For example, *The Bogleheads' Guide to Retirement Planning* is a wonderful resource, as is Jim Otar's *Unveiling the Retirement Myth*.

So why did I decide to write another? How does this book hope to be better than all of those other books?

It doesn't. *Can I Retire?* is not intended to be better. It's intended to be shorter. It's written for the person who might not be able to find the time to read Otar's entire 525-page book or the 370-page *Bogleheads' Guide*.

If you're considering reading a more in-depth guide to retirement planning, I wholeheartedly encourage you to do so. But if there's a good chance that, if you were to buy one of those other books, it would sit unread on your coffee table or bookshelf, then this book is written for you.

Retirement Planning: Create a Plan!

The goal of retirement planning is to create a plan. It feels silly to come out and say that, but from what I've seen, most investors never actually take the step of creating a concrete plan. Instead, they read a few articles about various retirement planning topics and they leave it at that. (And many investors don't even do that much.)

The more specifically you've planned how you'll manage your portfolio—and your finances in general—the less likely it is that you'll have to go back to work or dramatically reduce your spending later in retirement.

Of course, a retirement plan isn't set in stone. Unexpected expenses come up, tax laws change, and investment returns are unpredictable. But having a concrete, well-thought-out plan will help you:

- Reduce the likelihood of investment mistakes, such as panicking and selling an investment at the wrong time,
- Avoid wasting money on taxes simply because you're unaware of the tax-saving strategies available to you, and
- Prepare your nest egg to withstand a myriad of risks including poor investment returns, inflation, and the possibility that you'll live far longer than you had expected.

What This Book Will Cover

This book is intended to help you answer two questions as a part of your retirement planning process:

1. How much money do I need saved before I can retire?
2. Once I am retired, how should I manage my portfolio to minimize the risk of outliving my money?

Naturally, we'll break both of those questions down into several important sub-topics. But as you can see, there are still many retirement planning issues that this book *won't* cover—things like whether or not you should buy long-term care insurance, what to look for in an LTC policy, when to begin taking social security benefits, when your spouse should begin taking benefits, and so on.

As such, I suggest supplementing the information you gain from this book with either:

o The services of a trustworthy, unbiased, well-informed financial advisor, or
o An ongoing program of self-education, should you decide to handle your investments on your own.

PART ONE

How Much Money Will I Need to Retire?

CHAPTER ONE

How Much Income Do You Need?

It all starts with that question. There's really no way around it.

If you want, you can cheat by using a popular rule of thumb such as, "In retirement, you'll need 75% of your pre-retirement income." But who can say whether that rule of thumb will actually hold true *for you*? Different people have different plans for retirement, and it's common sense that those different plans come with different price tags.

In short, unless you're comfortable with the idea of looking for work several years into retirement, there's no viable alternative to sitting down and calculating how much income *you* are going to need.

Calculating Your Expenses

Fortunately, such calculations aren't as difficult as you might think. A simple two-step process can get the job done:

1. Determine your current expenses.
2. Do your best to estimate how those expenses will change.

To get the most meaningful figure of your current expenses, be sure to look at the last full year rather than just the last few months. Yes, it's more work, but it prevents you from overlooking expenses that you only pay for once per year, such as certain insurance premiums or annual vacations.

To calculate your expenses over the last year, you'll need three things: credit card statements, bank statements, and your payroll stubs (for expenses like insurance that were deducted directly from your wages).

After tallying up your expenses for the last year, do your best to adjust for things that will change in retirement. For example:

o Saving for retirement: You won't need to do it anymore once you're retired.
o Mortgage payment: If it hasn't already, this will go away once you've paid off your mortgage completely.

- o Work-related expenses (dry cleaning and commuting costs, for instance) will mostly disappear.
- o Health insurance premiums: How will they change as you age, as you become ineligible for your plan at work, and as you become eligible for Medicare?
- o Entertainment costs: Do you plan to travel the world or do you anticipate spending time on a hobby that might even *earn* money?

Of course, most of the figures here will be estimates. That's OK. You don't need a precise, to-the-penny budget. Any estimate based on your own goals and needs is going to be more accurate than the amount recommended by a rule of thumb.

If you're still many years from retirement, remember that your goals can change significantly over time. While the idea of running a part-time business in retirement may sound fun to you right now, there's no guarantee that it will sound just as appealing when retirement actually rolls around. Takeaway: It's important to revisit these calculations from time to time as you get closer to retirement.

Adjusting for Inflation

If you're more than a few years away from retirement, it's important to remember to account for inflation when calculating your expected retirement expenses. What rate of inflation you should use for your calculations is anybody's guess, though. Today, some experts are predicting hyperinflation, while others are predicting *de*flation. The best I can tell you is that, historically, inflation in the U.S. has averaged a little over 3% per year.[1]

EXAMPLE: Carrie is 55. Her expenses over the last year were $42,000. After considering how her lifestyle will change in retirement, she estimates her annual retirement expenses to be $34,000 (measured in today's dollars).

 If Carrie plans to retire in ten years, and she expects inflation to average 3% per year over that period, she should plan for her annual retirement expenses to start at $45,693, calculated as $34,000 x $(1 + 0.03)^{10}$. (I have an easy-to-use calculator at www.obliviousinvestor.com/inflation that can do this calculation for you.)

Adjusting for Taxes

Of course, due to taxes, in order to cover a given amount of annual expenses, you're going to need a greater dollar amount of annual income.

EXAMPLE: Larry expects his annual retirement expenses to be around $40,000. Between state and Federal taxes, he expects to pay a combined average

---

[1] 3.24% from 1913-2009, according to the U.S. Department of Labor's Consumer Price Index.

tax rate in retirement of 15%. In order to cover his expenses, he'll need $47,059 of pre-tax income, calculated as $40,000 ÷ 0.85 (because 85% of his pre-tax income is what will be available to spend, given a 15% average tax rate).

Pensions, Social Security, and Other Income

When determining whether you've saved enough in order to retire, the goal isn't to determine how much income you need each year, but rather how much income you need each year *from your investments*. To arrive at that figure, subtract any other income that you expect to receive—Social Security benefits, pension income, a part-time job, etc.

For example, if you expect to need $45,000 of pre-tax income each year, and you expect to receive a total of $20,000 from Social Security and pension income, you only need to fund $25,000 each year with your savings.[1]

You should receive a Social Security State-ment each year providing an estimate of the Social Security benefits you could receive as a result of your earnings to date. If you haven't received such a

---

[1] Remember, if you have a pension that isn't adjusted for inflation, it will satisfy a smaller and smaller portion of your needs each year—thereby increasing the amount you'll need to fund with your investments.

statement recently (or if you can't find it), you can find the information online at: http://www.ssa.gov/planners/calculators.htm

Social Security planning strategies are beyond the scope of this book, but it's worth pointing out that the decision of when to start taking Social Security benefits is one worthy of serious consideration. Depending on your circumstances, it may be best to start taking benefits as soon as you're eligible, or it may be best to wait as long as you can. Or, it may be beneficial to claim *spousal* benefits as early as possible, then switch at a later age to claim *worker* benefits. For more information about Social Security planning, I suggest reading Larry Swedroe's *The Only Guide You'll Ever Need to the Right Financial Plan* and/or *The Bogleheads' Guide to Retirement Planning*.

Chapter 1 Simple Summary

- The first step to retirement planning is to estimate how much income you'll need per year in retirement.

- When calculating your annual expenses, be sure to use an entire year of data so that you don't miss any expenses that are only paid once per year.

- Remember to account for inflation and income taxes when calculating how much income you'll need from your portfolio.

- When calculating the income you'll need from your portfolio, remember to subtract any income you expect to receive from other sources—pensions, Social Security, etc.

- As you get closer and closer to retirement, it's worth revisiting these calculations. A tabulation of your expenses one year prior to retirement will be much more useful than data from ten years prior to retirement.

CHAPTER TWO

Safe Withdrawal Rates: The 4% "Rule"

After determining how much income you need your investments to provide each year, the next question is: How much savings will it take to provide the desired level of income?

The most commonly-given answer to this question involves yet another rule of thumb: The 4% Rule. This guideline comes from a study done by three professors at Trinity University, which found that if you plan on increasing the amount you withdraw from your portfolio each year in order to keep up with inflation, the most you can withdraw from your portfolio in the first year of a thirty-year retirement is 4%, unless you want to run a significant risk of running out of money.[1]

---

[1] You can find the text of the study online in several places by searching for its full title: "Retirement Savings: Choosing a Withdrawal Rate That Is Sustainable."

EXAMPLE: Susan retires with a $600,000 portfolio. According to the 4% Rule, she should be able to withdraw $24,000 from the portfolio in her first year of retirement, and increase her withdrawal each year in keeping with inflation.

It's Only a Guideline.

Like any rule of thumb, the 4% rule isn't a hard-and-fast rule, so much as a rough guideline. First, as with any study based on historical investment returns, it's only useful to the extent that future returns mimic past returns. And there's no guarantee that they will. Second, the original study didn't account for retirements that last longer than 30 years, so if a lengthier retirement is a possibility for you, it would be wise to consider a starting withdrawal rate below 4%. Third, the study assumes that you won't make any investing mistakes, such as panicking and selling during a crash or picking a mutual fund that underperforms the market.

Why Only 4%?

Given that the U.S. stock market has averaged an inflation-adjusted return of 8.1% from 1928-2009, many people are surprised at such a low suggested withdrawal rate. If the stock market averages an 8% return, why can't you plan to withdraw 8% of your portfolio per year? There are two reasons, and they're both related to the unpredictability of investment returns.

Volatility Is Bad News When Selling.

You've likely read about the virtues of dollar-cost-averaging (that is, making systematic purchases of an investment). The idea is that if you purchase a fixed dollar amount of a stock or mutual fund every month, you'll be buying more shares when the stock's price is low and fewer when it's high. In other words, you'll be automating the "buy low" part of the old adage to "buy low, sell high."

In retirement, however, the opposite is true. When you're retired, you're systematically *selling* your holdings rather than buying more. And if you're dollar-cost-averaging *out* of a volatile investment, you'll be selling more shares when the price is low and fewer shares when the price is high. This is not a good thing.

The takeaway here is that once you begin liquidating your investments, volatility takes on a whole new significance: It directly reduces your returns. So even if the stock market earns a specific return over the course of your retirement, it's likely that your own stock portfolio (even if it's held in index funds that track the market) will earn a lesser return due to the return-damaging effect of dollar-cost-averaging *out* of a volatile investment.

Sequence of Returns Risk (a.k.a. "Luck")

"Sequence of returns risk" is the second reason that it's not safe to withdraw 8% per year even if you expect your portfolio to earn an average return of 8% per year throughout your retirement. It's a fancy term, but all it really means is this: The *order* in which returns occur matters a great deal.

Specifically, when you're systematically taking money *out* of an investment portfolio, the early returns (i.e., the ones that occur while you still have a lot of money invested) are the ones that matter most.

If you're withdrawing more than a few percent of your portfolio per year, and you experience a severe or extended bear market early in retirement, there might not be enough of your portfolio left for your retirement to be saved when the market finally does rebound.

EXAMPLE: Agnes retires in 2011 with a $400,000 portfolio, from which she takes $15,000 at the beginning of each year. Over the first five years of her retirement, her portfolio earns the following annual returns: 15%, 12%, 3%, -6%, -12%.

Her portfolio values at the end of each year will be as follows:

- o 2011: $442,750
- o 2012: $479,080
- o 2013: $478,002
- o 2014: $435,222
- o 2015: $369,796.

If, however, the returns had occurred in the opposite order, her portfolio value would look as follows:

- o 2011: $338,800
- o 2012: $304,372
- o 2013: $298,053
- o 2014: $317,020
- o 2015: $347,322

That's a difference of more than $22,000 in ending value—just because the returns occurred in a different *order*. As you'll note, the scenario in which the good returns occurred first turned out better for Agnes. That's because, when you're withdrawing money, the earlier returns have a greater impact than the later returns.

To see how big an effect the sequence of returns can have over the course of your retirement, imagine the case of an investor who retires with a $500,000 portfolio, invested 50% in stocks, 50% in bonds, and rebalanced annually. She uses a starting withdrawal rate of 6%, which she then adjusts upward to keep up with inflation.

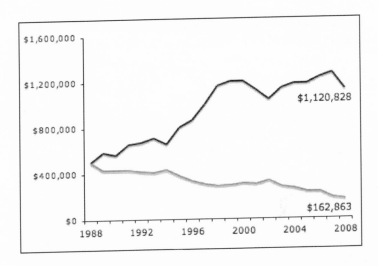

The top line shows what would have happened if the investor retired at the end of 1988, right before the roaring bull market of the 90s. Twenty years into her retirement, her portfolio value would have more than doubled to $1,120,828.

But what's that line at the bottom? That line indicates what would have happened if those twenty years of returns had occurred in the opposite order. In that scenario, the investor's portfolio has declined to $162,863, and will probably only last a few more years.

That's a huge difference! Twenty years into retirement, you could be a millionaire, or rapidly approaching broke, depending solely upon the *order* in which your investment returns occur—something over which you have no control.

With unpredictable investments, there's no way to eliminate sequence of returns risk. But if you

13

use a low withdrawal rate, you can at least reduce the possibility of going broke simply due to an unlucky order of returns.

Chapter 2 Simple Summary

- 4% is typically thought to be the highest starting withdrawal rate that you can use for a 30-year retirement, unless you want to run a significant risk of outliving your savings.

- The 4% "rule" is only a guideline. There's no guarantee that it will work, especially if your retirement may be longer than 30 years.

- Because of the negative effects of volatility and inflation, it's important to use a starting withdrawal rate that's *lower* than the return you expect to earn on your portfolio.

CHAPTER THREE

What if 4% Isn't Enough?

In order to retire with a 4% withdrawal rate, your retirement portfolio must be 25-times your annual pre-tax income needs.[1] So if you need, for example, $35,000 of pre-tax income from your investments, you'd need to save $875,000 before you can retire. (And as we mentioned in the previous chapter, there's no guarantee that even a 4% withdrawal rate is low enough to be safe.)

Unfortunately, for many investors nearing retirement age, saving 25-times their necessary investment income just isn't going to happen. They're too close to retirement—and too far away from that goal—for it to be possible.

If you're in such a situation, there are five primary options for getting your retirement savings to where they need to be:

---

[1] Because $1 \div 0.04 = 25$.

1. Cut your expenses now (so you can save more each year),
2. Cut your planned expenses in retirement,
3. Work part-time during retirement,
4. Retire later than you originally planned, or
5. Annuitize a portion of your portfolio.

Each of these methods *will* get you closer to the amount of money necessary for retiring safely. But they all involve making sacrifices, and that's never popular. (And most investors have never heard of option #5 anyway.[1]) As a result, many investors try to create an option #6: Aim for higher investment returns so that your portfolio will grow faster between now and retirement

Increasing Returns is No Easy Task.

The most common approaches to seeking higher returns are to:

1. Include a heavier stock allocation in your portfolio, or
2. Attempt to outperform the market.

Increasing your stock allocation in an attempt to increase returns might work. Or, it might not. While stocks have historically earned greater returns than

---

[1] Using annuities to achieve a higher withdrawal rate is the subject of the next chapter.

bonds, there's absolutely no guarantee that they'll outperform bonds (or earn a positive return at all, for that matter) over any particular period. Moving more of your money into stocks shortly before retirement is a risky strategy.

Similarly, attempting to earn above-market returns has the potential to backfire. It's not impossible—after all, a randomly-selected portfolio of stocks has a 50% chance of outperforming the market—but it's one heck of a feat to be able to do it reliably.

In fact, even the pros can't seem to get the job done consistently. According to a study done by Standard and Poors[1], for the five years ending December 31, 2009, less than 40% of stock mutual funds managed to outperform their respective benchmarks. And that's not a fluke. Standard and Poors has been doing this study for years, and it consistently shows the same thing: Even the professionals have less than a 50% chance of beating the stock market.[2]

If you have no reason to think that you have a meaningful advantage over the professionals—and I would argue that most investors do not—then the only reliable answer is to adjust your plans. Figure out a way to make your retirement work without

---

[1] Available at:
www.standardandpoors.com/indices/spiva/en/us
[2] This is why I advocate investing via low-cost index funds that seek only to *match* the market's return. We'll discuss that topic a bit more in Chapter 5.

earning superstar investment returns, whether that
means retiring later, working part-time in retirement, cutting your expenses, or (as we'll discuss
next) annuitizing a part of your portfolio.

Chapter 3 Simple Summary

- If a 4% withdrawal rate isn't high enough to
  satisfy your goals, your best bet is to cut your
  spending or postpone retirement.

- Increasing your stock allocation in an attempt
  to earn higher returns can backfire. Stock returns are simply not predictable over any particular period.

- Reliably earning above-market returns is extremely difficult. Attempting to do so involves
  taking on a significant risk of *under*perform-
  ing the market.

Retirement Planning with Annuities

Many annuities (maybe even most) are a raw deal for investors. They carry needlessly high expenses and surrender charges, and their contracts are so complex that very few investors can properly assess whether the annuity is a good investment.

That said, one specific type of annuity can be an extremely useful tool for retirement planning: the single premium immediate annuity (SPIA).

What's an SPIA?

A single premium immediate annuity is a contract with an insurance company whereby:

1. You pay them a sum of money up front (known as a premium), and

2. They promise to pay you a certain amount of money periodically (monthly, for instance) for the rest of your life.[1]

For some annuities, the payout is a fixed amount each period—making for a single premium immediate *fixed* annuity.

For other annuities, the payout is linked to the performance of a mutual fund—making for a single premium immediate *variable* annuity. For the most part, I'd suggest steering clear of variable annuities. They tend to be complex and expensive. And because they each offer different bells and whistles, it's difficult to make comparisons between annuity providers to see which one offers the best deal.

In contrast, fixed SPIAs are helpful tools for two reasons:

1. They make retirement planning easier, and
2. They allow for a higher withdrawal rate than you can *safely* take from a portfolio of stocks, bonds, and mutual funds over the course of a potentially-lengthy retirement.

Note: It's possible to buy a fixed SPIA with a payout that adjusts upward each year in keeping with

---

[1] There are also some SPIAs that only pay out for a fixed period, rather than for the rest of your life. However, for the purposes of this book, when I use the term SPIA, I'm referring to a lifetime annuity.

inflation. This inflation protection isn't free, how-ever. Inflation-adjusted fixed annuities require higher initial premiums than fixed annuities without an inflation adjustment.

Retirement Planning with SPIAs

Fixed SPIAs make retirement planning easier in exactly the same way that traditional pensions do: They're predictable. If you know that you need $X of income each year in retirement, you can go to an online annuity quote provider, put in $X as the payout, check "yes" for inflation adjustments, and you'll get an answer: "For $Y, you can purchase an annuity that will pay you $X per year, adjusted for inflation, for the rest of your life—no matter how long you might live."[1]

Pretty easy, right? You now have a specific figure for the minimum amount of savings necessary to retire safely.

With a traditional stock and bond portfolio, retirement planning is more of a guessing game. There are whole books written on the subject of how to determine how large your stock/bond portfolio must be in order to retire safely.

---

[1] In order to get the most meaningful figure, be sure to get a quote for an SPIA with a payout linked to the consumer price index, rather than one that simply promises a fixed percentage increase from year to year.

SPIAs and Withdrawal Rates

Fixed SPIAs are also helpful because they allow you to retire on less money than you would need with a typical stock/bond portfolio. For example, as of this writing, according to Vanguard's online SPIA quote provider[1], a 65-year-old male could purchase an inflation-indexed annuity paying 5.56% annually.

If that investor were to take a withdrawal rate of 5.56% from a typical stock/bond portfolio, then adjust the withdrawal upward each year for inflation, there's a meaningful chance that he'd run out of money during his lifetime. That risk disappears with an annuity.

How is that possible? In short, it's possible because the annuitant gives up the right to keep the money once he dies. If you buy an SPIA and die the next day, the money is gone.[2] Your heirs don't get to keep it—the insurance company does. And the insurance company uses (most of) that money to fund the payouts on SPIAs purchased by people who are still living.

---

[1] Available at:

http://vanguard.com/us/whatweoffer/annuities/income

[2] There are some exceptions. For example, you can buy an SPIA that promises to pay income for the *longer* of your lifetime or a given number of years. But purchasing such an add-on reduces the payout, thereby reducing the ability of the SPIA to do what it does so well—provide a darned-high payout with very little risk.

In essence, SPIA purchasers who die before their life expectancy end up funding the retirement of SPIA purchasers who live past their life expectancy.

But I Want to Leave Something to My Heirs!

For many people, knowing that the money used to purchase an annuity will not go to their heirs is a deal breaker. And that's OK. It's perfectly natural to want to leave something to your kids or other loved ones.

The important takeaway here is that *if* your retirement may last thirty years or more, and *if* your savings are of a size such that you'd need to use a withdrawal rate much higher than 4%, you may not have much of a choice. If you choose not to annuitize—in the hope of leaving more to your kids—the decision could backfire. You could run out of money while you're still alive, thereby becoming a financial burden on your kids.

What Portion of Your Portfolio to Annuitize

Even if you had no desire whatsoever to leave anything to your heirs, it would still be unwise to annuitize your entire portfolio. The reason is that annuities cannot easily be sold. And since it's always possible that you'll be faced with a sudden, large expense, it's usually best to keep a portion of your portfolio in liquid assets: Stocks, bonds, cash, and so on.

So how much of your portfolio *should* you devote to an annuity? Let's look at an example.

EXAMPLE: Greg is a 65-year-old male investor with a $600,000 portfolio. To fund his lifestyle, Greg plans to withdraw $30,000 in his first year of retirement and adjust that amount upward each year for inflation.

In other words, Greg wants to use a 5% withdrawal rate ($30,000 ÷ $600,000 = 5%). That's more than most financial planners would recommend for a non-annuitized portfolio.

If we assume that Greg is comfortable using a 4% withdrawal rate for the non-annuitized portion of his portfolio, and we use the annuity quote from Vanguard mentioned on page 22 (a 5.56% payout for a 65-year-old male), we can calculate the amount Greg should annuitize (A) as follows:

$$0.0556 \times A + 0.04 \times (600,000 - A) = 30,000^1$$

If we solve for A, we get $384,615. This tells us that, if Greg a) buys the annuity at age 65 and b) doesn't want to use a withdrawal rate higher than 4% on the

---

[1] I have an online calculator that can do this math for you. It's available at: www.obliviousinvestor.com/annuitization-calculator/

non-annuitized part of his portfolio, he must put $384,615 of his $600,000 portfolio into the annuity in order to provide $30,000 of income each year.

But should Greg purchase the annuity at age 65, or should he wait?

When to Purchase an Annuity

Again, using Vanguard's quote page[1], we can see that for a 65-year-old male:

- ○ If you buy, for example, a $100,000 annuity now, you'll get a monthly income of $463 (which adjusts upward for inflation) for the remainder of your life.
- ○ But if you wait to age 66, an annuity paying $463/month would only cost $95,673.

Therefore, you're better off waiting if you believe that, between ages 65 and 66, you can invest that $100,000 on your own and, while spending $463 per month, have $95,673 or more left (after adjusting for inflation) when you turn 66. Doing so would require an after-inflation annual return of approximately 1.25%.

---

[1] http://vanguard.com/us/whatweoffer/annuities/income

The Role of Interest Rates

The prior analysis assumes that the payout for an immediate fixed annuity for a 66-year-old one year from now will be the same as the quote for somebody who is 66 today. Unfortunately, that's not entirely true.

Annuity payouts and premiums change as a function of market interest rates. When market interest rates are higher, annuity payouts are higher as well, because the insurance company knows that it can invest your money at a higher rate of return and can, therefore, offer to pay you a higher rate.

So the decision to delay is a function not only of what inflation-adjusted rate of return you think you could earn over the period in question, but also of where you think interest rates are headed next. If you expect interest rates to rise, delaying annuitization is more attractive than if you expect interest rates to decline.

Annuity Income: Is It Safe?

Because the income from an annuity is backed by an insurance company, financial advisors and financial literature usually refer to it as "guaranteed."

But that doesn't mean it's a 100% sure-thing. Just like any company, insurance companies can go belly-up. It's not common, but it's certainly not impossible, especially given that:

1. The longer the period in question, the greater the likelihood of any given company going out of business, and
2. The entire point of an annuity is to protect you against longevity risk (that is, the risk that you last longer than your money). So presumably, we're talking about a fairly long period of time.

However, if you're careful, the possibility of your annuity provider going out of business doesn't have to keep you up at night.

Check Your Insurance Company's Financial Strength

Before placing a meaningful portion of your retirement savings in the hands of an insurance company, it's important to check that company's financial strength. I'd suggest checking with multiple ratings agencies, for example:

o   Standard and Poor's
o   Moody's
o   A.M. Best

State Guarantee Associations

Even if the issuer of your annuity *does* go bankrupt, you aren't necessarily in trouble. Each state has a guarantee association (funded by the insurance companies themselves) that will step in if your insurance company goes insolvent.

It's important to note, however, that the state guarantee associations only provide coverage up to a certain limit. And that limit varies from state to state. Equally important: The rules regarding the coverage vary from state to state.

For example, Arkansas provides coverage of up to $300,000 per annuitant, per insurance company insolvency. But they only provide coverage to investors who are residents of Arkansas at the time the insurance company becomes insolvent. So if you have an annuity currently worth $300,000, and you move to Illinois (where the coverage is capped at $100,000), you're putting your money at risk.

In contrast, New York offers $500,000 of coverage, and they cover you if you are a NY state resident either when the insurance company goes insolvent *or* when the annuity was issued. So moving to another state with a lower coverage limit isn't a problem if you bought your annuity in New York.

Minimizing Your Risk

In short, annuities can be a very useful tool for minimizing the risk that you'll run out of money in retirement. But to maximize the likelihood that you'll receive the promised payout, it's important to take the following steps:

1. Check the financial strength of the insurance company before purchasing an annuity.
2. Know the limit for guarantee association coverage in your state as well as the rules accompanying such coverage.
3. Consider diversifying between insurance companies. For instance, if your state's guarantee association only provides coverage up to $100,000 and you want to annuitize $300,000 of your portfolio, consider buying a $100,00 annuity from each of three different insurance companies.
4. Before moving from one state to another, be sure to check the guarantee association coverage in your new state to make sure you're not putting your standard of living at risk.

Chapter 4 Simple Summary

- Single premium immediate fixed annuities can be helpful because they allow for a higher withdrawal rate than would be sustainable from a typical portfolio of other investments.

- In exchange for this increased safe withdrawal rate, you give up control of the money as well as the possibility of leaving the money to your heirs.

- The decision of when to purchase an annuity is a function of the rate of return you would earn on a non-annuitized portfolio, the rate at which annuity payouts increase with age, and the direction in which you believe interest rates are headed.

- Before buying an annuity, check the financial strength of the insurance company and make sure you're familiar with the rules and coverage limits for your state's guarantee association.

PART TWO

Managing a Retirement-Stage Portfolio

By this point, we've discussed how much money you need to save in order to retire and the role annuities can play in (safely) increasing the amount of income that your portfolio provides. In this next section, we'll discuss strategies for managing the *non*-annuitized portion of your portfolio so as to minimize the risk of outliving your money.

31

Index Funds and ETFs

Index funds are mutual funds designed to track a specific index (the S&P 500, for instance). This is in contrast to most mutual funds, which are run by fund managers seeking to *beat* a given index (i.e., earn above average returns) rather than just *match* it.[1]

Because index funds seek only to mimic an index, they can be run for significantly lower costs than other, actively managed mutual funds. For example, the typical U.S. stock mutual fund carries an expense ratio of roughly 1%, whereas it's easy to find stock index funds charging 0.2% or less.

Study after study has shown that low-cost mutual funds tend to outperform high-cost funds. For example, a recent Morningstar study found that, for the five-year period ending 3/31/2010, the

---

[1] An index is simply a number that tracks the price of certain investments. The S&P 500, for instance, tracks the price of 500 large U.S. companies.

cheapest quintile of funds outperformed the most expensive quintile of funds in every single asset class.[1] This shouldn't be any surprise, really. The less a fund charges, the more returns there are for fund investors to take home.

An additional advantage of index funds is that many of them are very broadly diversified. For example:

- An index fund tracking the *Wilshire 5000 Total Market Index* would own thousands of U.S. companies,
- An index fund tracking the *FTSE All-World ex US Index* would own over 2,000 different international companies, and
- An index fund tracking the *Barclay's Capital U.S. Aggregate Bond Index* would own approximately 3,000 different bonds from a wide variety of borrowers.

In other words, by buying just three index funds, you could have a portfolio consisting of thousands of companies from across the globe, as well as a broadly diversified collection of bonds.

One final benefit of index funds is that they have no "management risk." That is, you don't have to worry that your superstar fund manager will quit to go to a different firm or that your fund manager

---

[1] You'll have to register for a free account to view it, but you can find more info about the study on Morningstar's website at:
news.morningstar.com/articlenet/article.aspx?id=347327

will place a large, unlucky bet on a particular stock (or industry, or country) and that you won't find out about it until it's too late.

Exchange Traded Funds (ETFs)

ETFs are essentially index funds that are bought and sold like regular stocks rather than like mutual funds.[1] Among other things (most of which aren't important for the typical buy & hold investor), the fact that ETFs trade like stocks means that ETFs can be purchased via any brokerage firm, whereas many index funds must be purchased via an account with the company that runs the fund (unless you want to pay a commission on every purchase).

For buy and hold investors, the biggest differences between ETFs and index funds are that ETFs typically carry slightly lower expense ratios, but buying or selling them involves paying two costs. The first is a brokerage commission, typically in the range of $5-10 per trade. (Exception: Vanguard, Fidelity, and Schwab each have arrangements allowing investors to buy and sell certain ETFs without paying any trade commissions.)

---

[1] There are also some ETFs that are more akin to actively managed mutual funds than to index funds. For the purposes of this book, however, when I say "ETF," I'm referring to ETFs that, like index funds, are low-cost and track a specific index.

The second cost is the "bid/ask spread," which refers to the difference between the lowest price at which you can *buy* the ETF and the highest price at which you can *sell* the ETF.

EXAMPLE: As I write this, Vanguard's Small-Cap ETF *costs* $65.18 per share to buy. However, the highest price that anybody is currently *offering* is $65.14, which means that $65.14 is the most you could get if you wanted to *sell* a share of the ETF. As such, if you bought 100 shares of the ETF, then turned around and sold them immediately, you'd lose $4 ($0.04 x 100 shares) on the transaction (in addition to any brokerage commissions you might pay).

For the most part though, as long as you stick with well-known, highly-traded ETFs, your spread cost will be relatively minor (often as little as $0.01 per share).

Chapter 5 Simple Summary

- One of the most reliable ways to find top-performing funds is to look for funds with very low costs.

- Because of their low costs, broad diversification, and transparency, index funds and ETFs are excellent tools for constructing a buy and hold portfolio.

- ETFs typically have slightly lower operating expenses than index funds, but buying or selling them often involves paying a commission.

- Unless your brokerage firm offers commission-free ETF trades, you may want to stick with traditional index funds if you expect to be making frequent transactions, such as liquidating a portion of your holdings each month.

CHAPTER SIX

401(k) Rollovers

After leaving your job, you'll have to decide whether or not you want to roll your 401(k) into an IRA. For the most part, the answer is easy: Yes, roll over your 401(k).[1]

Better Investment Options in an IRA

There's no question that reducing your investment costs is one of the most reliable ways to improve your investment returns. Unfortunately, many 401(k) plans have only one low-cost investment option: an S&P 500 index fund. (And some plans don't even have that!) This forces you to either:

---

[1] I use the term 401(k) throughout this chapter, though a very similar analysis would apply to a different employer-sponsored retirement plan, such as a 403(b) or 457(b).

- Use high-cost mutual funds for the remaining portions of your portfolio (bonds, international stocks, small cap stocks, etc.), or
- Keep an inappropriately large holding of the S&P 500 index fund in order to keep costs down (thereby throwing your asset allocation out of whack).[1]

In contrast, with an IRA, you'll have access to a wide array of low-cost investment options in every asset class.

Lower Fees in an IRA

In addition to limiting you to high-cost funds, most 401(k) plans include an (often hidden) administrative fee. A 2009 study by Deloitte and the Investment Company Institute found the median administrative fee to be 0.72% of assets annually. In contrast, many brokerage firms charge no annual IRA fees at all.

Between less expensive investment options and lower administrative costs, it's likely that you can reduce your total investment costs by 1% per year simply by moving your money from a 401(k) to an IRA. That might not sound like much, but when compounded over your whole retirement, improving

---

[1] One noteworthy exception is the Federal Thrift Savings Plan. Federal employees with access to the TSP can build an *extremely* low-cost diversified portfolio without needing to take their money anywhere else.

your investment return by 1% can have a dramatic impact on how long your money lasts.

Try thinking of it this way: Incurring investment costs of 1% per year changes a 4% withdrawal rate (fairly safe over a normal-length retirement) into a 5% withdrawal rate (not safe over a normal-length retirement). Or, to look at it yet another way, if you plan to use a 4% withdrawal rate, paying investment costs of 1% per year would mean that you can only actually *spend* 3% of your portfolio value—that's a 25% reduction in your ability to spend!

Reasons *Not* to Roll Over a 401(k)

There are, however, a few specific situations in which it doesn't make sense to roll over a 401(k)—or other employer-sponsored retirement plan—after leaving your job.

If you are "separated from service" (i.e., you leave your job, were laid off, etc.) at age 55 or later, distributions from your 401(k) will not be subject to the 10% additional tax that normally comes with retirement account distributions before age 59½.

As a result, if you are 55 or older when you leave your job and you plan to retire prior to age 59½, it may make sense to put off rolling your 401(k) into an IRA until you *are* 59½. This way, if you need to spend some of the money prior to age 59½, you can do so without having to worry about the 10% additional tax.

Alternatively, if you currently have a traditional IRA to which you made non-deductible contributions and you are planning a Roth conversion, you may want to hold off on rolling over your 401(k) until the year after you've executed the Roth conversion, so as to minimize the portion of the conversion that's taxable.[1]

Lastly, if your 401(k) includes employer stock that has significantly appreciated in value from the time you purchased it, you'd do well to speak with an accountant before rolling over your 401(k). Why? Because under the "Net Unrealized Appreciation" rules, you may be able to take a lump-sum distribution of your 401(k) account, moving the employer stock into a taxable account and rolling the rest of the account into an IRA.

Why would such a maneuver be beneficial? Because, if you roll the stock into a taxable account, only your basis in the stock (i.e., the amount you paid for it) will be taxed as a distribution. The amount by which the shares have appreciated in value (the "Net Unrealized Appreciation") isn't taxed until you sell the stock. And even then, it will be taxed at long-term capital gain tax rates (currently, a max of 15%) instead of being taxed as ordinary income.[2]

In contrast, if you roll the stock into an IRA, when you withdraw the money from the IRA, the

---

[1] Roth conversions are the subject of Chapter 9, so don't worry if this doesn't make much sense right now.

[2] If the stock is sold within one year of the date of the distribution, any gain attributable to an increase in the price of the stock since the date of the distribution will be taxed as a short-term capital gain.

entire amount will count as ordinary income and will be taxed according to your ordinary income tax bracket at the time of withdrawal.

EXAMPLE: Martha recently retired from her job with a utility company. She owns employer stock in her 401(k). The stock is currently worth $100,000. The total amount she paid for the shares was $42,000.

If she rolls her entire 401(k) into an IRA, when she withdraws that $100,000, the entire amount will be taxable as ordinary income.

If, however, she rolls the employer stock into a taxable account, she'll only be taxed upon her basis in the shares ($42,000). And when she eventually sells the shares, the gain will be taxed as a long-term capital gain (at a maximum rate of 15%) rather than as ordinary income.

Remember, though, that holding a significant amount of your net worth in one company's stock is risky—*especially when that company is your employer*. Be careful not to take on too much risk in your 401(k) solely in the hope of getting a tax benefit in the future.

And to reiterate, if you think you might benefit from the Net Unrealized Appreciation rules, it's definitely a good idea to speak with a tax professional to ensure that you execute the procedure properly.

How to Roll Over a 401(k)

In most cases, rolling over a 401(k) is just four easy steps:

1. Open a traditional IRA if you don't already have one,
2. Request rollover paperwork from your plan administrator,
3. Fill out the paperwork and send it back in, and
4. Once the money has arrived in your IRA, go ahead and invest it as you see fit.

When you're filling out the paperwork, you'll want to initiate a "direct rollover" (sometimes called a "trustee-to-trustee" rollover). That is, do not have the check made out to you. Have it made out to—and sent to—the new brokerage firm.

If for some reason the check arrives in your own mailbox, don't panic. But be sure to forward the check to the new brokerage firm ASAP. If you don't get it rolled over into your new IRA within 60 days, the entire amount will count as a taxable distribution this year, which would likely result in a hefty tax bill.

Where to Roll Over Your 401(k)

In terms of where to roll over your 401(k), you have three major options. You can roll your 401(k) account into an IRA account[1] at:

1. A mutual fund company,
2. A discount brokerage firm, or
3. A full service brokerage firm.

Rolling a 401(k) into an IRA account with a mutual fund company can be a good choice. As long as you make sure to choose a fund company that has low-cost funds, low (or no) administrative fees for IRAs, and a broad enough selection of funds to build a diversified portfolio, you should do just fine. For example, Vanguard has excellent index funds and would be a great place to roll over a 401(k).

Your second option is to roll your 401(k) account into an IRA account at a discount brokerage firm, such as Charles Schwab or Fidelity. Due to the proliferation of exchange-traded funds (ETFs), you

---

[1] Believe it or not, the term "IRA account" is not redundant. IRA actually stands for "Individual Retirement Arrangement." As far as the IRS is concerned, you only have one IRA. That IRA may, however, be made up of multiple IRA *accounts* at various brokerage firms. This distinction is significant because some tax provisions apply to your entire IRA while others apply only to a specific IRA *account*.

43

can now quickly and easily create a low-cost, diversified portfolio at any discount brokerage firm.[1]

Option #3—using a "full service" brokerage firm—is one I'd generally recommend against. At these companies, brokers (calling themselves Financial Advisors) make a living by repeating this process:

1. Track down somebody with a 401(k) account to roll over,
2. Convince him to roll it into an IRA account at their firm, and
3. Once it's rolled over, sell the investor a portfolio of mutual funds with steep up-front sales loads.

To name names: At companies like Morgan Stanley Smith Barney, Merrill Lynch, Wachovia, UBS, or Edward Jones, a financial advisor will usually try to sell you a portfolio of funds with front-end commissions (a needless cost) or an advisory account with unnecessarily high ongoing fees.[2]

---

[1] And, as mentioned in the previous chapter, Schwab, Fidelity, and Vanguard now offer commission-free trades on certain ETFs.

[2] The same thing goes for rolling a 401(k) into an IRA account with an insurance company or a bank. In most cases, you'll be working with a commission-paid salesperson whose job is to sell you high-cost investments.

Chapter 6 Simple Summary

- In most cases, it's beneficial to roll your 401(k) into an IRA after leaving your job. Doing so will give you access to better investment options and will likely reduce your administrative costs as well.

- If you left your job at age 55 or older, and you plan to retire prior to age 59½, you may want to postpone rolling over your 401(k) until you reach age 59½.

- If you're planning a Roth conversion of non-deductible IRA contributions, you may want to hold off on a 401(k) rollover until the year after your Roth conversion is complete.

- If you have employer stock in your 401(k), before rolling your 401(k) into an IRA, it's probably a good idea to speak with an accountant to see if you can take advantage of the Net Unrealized Appreciation rules.

- In most cases, the best place to roll over a 401(k) is a mutual fund company with low-cost funds or a discount brokerage firm that offers low-cost (or no-cost) trades on ETFs.

CHAPTER SEVEN

Asset Allocation for Retirement Portfolios

When you're still working, the appropriate response to a market decline is usually just to refrain from panicking and selling. Once you're retired, however, that's not always an option. You need cash to pay your bills, and if it has to come from your investments, it has to come from your investments—no matter how poorly they've performed recently.

As a result, if your portfolio is invested too aggressively, a poorly timed bear market (i.e., one at the beginning of your retirement) can be crushing because you'll be forced to sell a large portion of your portfolio at precisely the worst time.

In addition, as mentioned in Chapter 2, volatility has another detrimental effect on a retirement portfolio: Since you're dollar-cost-averaging *out* of your investments, volatility directly reduces your returns.

But, despite the double-pronged danger that volatility poses for a retirement portfolio, most investors can't ditch all their stock holdings in favor of CDs and short-term bonds without facing the risk of being overrun by inflation at some point in retirement.

So what's an investor to do? How should you go about balancing the need for low volatility with the need to outpace inflation?

The "Age in Bonds" Method

A popular asset allocation method is to set your bond allocation equal to your age. So, for example, if you're 65 now, 65% of your portfolio would be in bonds, and 35% would be in stocks.

Such a guideline is reasonable, as far as it goes. But that's just the problem: It doesn't go far enough. To create an actual plan for managing your portfolio, you'll need to get more specific. Among other things, you'll have to determine:

o   How you want to allocate the bond portion of your portfolio among various types of bonds,
o   How you want to allocate the stock portion of your portfolio among various categories of stocks, and
o   How, specifically, you plan to go about liquidating your portfolio. For example, how will you decide which investments to sell to raise cash? And how often will you do that? And

how often will you "rebalance" the rest of your portfolio back to your desired asset allocation?

Anybody's Guess

The unfortunate truth about asset allocation is that nobody can say ahead of time which allocation is best. We can look at historical data and draw conclusions about what allocations and strategies have worked well in the past, but it's far from certain that the same strategies will be optimal for the future.

As a result, two well-informed investors could choose two very different asset allocation strategies. All of this is to say that what follows is my own suggestion, but it is not, by any means, the only reasonable approach to asset allocation in retirement.

The "Buckets" Method

Using this method[1], you separate your portfolio into three separate portfolios ("buckets"):

1. **The spending bucket:** Two years of living expenses kept in a money market, savings, or interest-bearing checking account,

---

[1] Adapted from a method discussed in Jim Otar's insightful book, *Unveiling the Retirement Myth*.

2. **The intermediate bucket:** Three years of living expenses kept in short-term Treasury bonds (or a low-cost short-term Treasury ETF or index fund), and

3. **The long-term bucket:** The remainder of the portfolio, uses a static, conservative allocation (50% stocks, 50% bonds, for example).[1]

The idea is to invest each dollar appropriately given the length of time before it will be spent. So, any money to be spent in the very near future (two years or less) must be kept in something with essentially zero risk, such as a savings account. Money intended to be spent between 3-5 years from now can have a little more risk, but still not much, hence the use of short-term Treasury bonds. And money to be spent in the more distant future is where we can afford to take the most risk, hence the use of stocks and longer-term bonds.

Rebalancing Your Buckets

Rebalancing is the process of adjusting your holdings to bring them back to your ideal asset allocation. Since your two low-risk buckets only have one holding each, there's nothing to rebalance. Your

---

[1] How to allocate this long-term bucket is the subject of the next chapter.

long-term bucket, however, will have to be rebalanced at some point. But when? And how often?

To date, the best answer I've seen to the question of how often to rebalance is that put forth by William Bernstein in his book *The Four Pillars of Investing*. Bernstein points out that the ideal frequency for rebalancing is the one that gives the stock market enough time to run through one half of a bear/bull cycle. (In other words, the best time to sell a portion of your stock holdings and move more heavily into bonds would, naturally, be near the end of a bull market in stocks.)

As Bernstein reminds us, however, the length of bull and bear markets varies considerably. For the most part though, bear markets and bull markets tend to last for periods of greater than one year. As a result, rebalancing more frequently than once per year is likely to be harmful to performance.[1]

When to Refill Your Buckets

Clearly, the spending and intermediate buckets must be refilled at some point with money from the long-term bucket. But how frequently should you do so?

Many investors do it on an ongoing basis— constantly refilling the spending bucket with money

---

[1] If a substantial portion of your assets is held in taxable accounts, frequent rebalancing becomes even less desirable as it often comes with an additional cost in the form of taxable capital gains.

from the intermediate bucket and refilling the intermediate bucket with money from the long-term bucket. But if you do that, you may as well be spending from the long-term bucket!

In other words, the problem with constantly selling your stocks and long-term bonds to replenish your two low-risk buckets is that it almost negates the point of *having* the two low-risk buckets. It leaves you with the return-damaging effects of dollar-cost-averaging out of volatile investments. And it leaves you exposed to the risk of selling your stock holdings throughout a bear market.

Instead, my suggestion is to:

o Frequently refill the spending bucket with money from the intermediate bucket,

o Set your accounts up so that interest and dividends received in your long-term bucket are automatically used to refill your spending bucket, and

o Completely refill your spending and intermediate buckets (with money from the long-term bucket) whenever you rebalance your long-term bucket (so, as we just discussed, every couple years perhaps).

EXAMPLE: When Bill retires, his portfolio is worth $600,000, and he needs it to provide $24,000 of income per year. Bill has decided that a 50% stock, 50% bond allocation is appropriate for his long-term bucket. At the moment, Bill's buckets look like this:

- o Spending bucket: $48,000 ($24,000 x 2) in a money market account.
- o Intermediate bucket: $72,000 ($24,000 x 3) in short-term Treasury bonds.
- o Long-term bucket: $240,000 in bonds and $240,000 in stocks.

After two years of retirement, however, he's spent some money and his investments have changed in value, so his buckets now look like this:

- o Spending bucket: $48,000 in money market (because Bill has been filling it regularly with money from his intermediate bucket)
- o Intermediate bucket: $35,000 in short-term Treasury bonds
- o Long-term bucket: $220,000 in bonds, $300,000 in stocks.

To replenish his intermediate bucket, Bill will sell $37,000 of stocks and buy short-term Treasury bonds, thereby bringing the total for that bucket back up to $72,000.

That will leave him with $220,000 of bonds and $263,000 of stocks in his long-term bucket. To bring it back to a 50/50 allocation, Bill should move $21,500 from stocks into bonds.

Chapter 7 Simple Summary

- We can use historical data to make educated guesses about what might be wise or unwise, but there's no "right" answer to asset allocation.

- By keeping significant holdings of very low-risk investments, such as cash and short-term Treasury bonds, you reduce the harmful effects of dollar-cost-averaging out of volatile investments.

- Rebalancing your long-term bucket more than once per year is likely to be detrimental to returns.

- Hold off on using your long-term bucket to refill the two low-risk buckets until it's time to rebalance your long-term bucket.

CHAPTER EIGHT

Asset Allocation Part 2:
Allocating Your Long-Term Bucket

We've determined that bucket #3 can take somewhat higher risk than the other two buckets, and that it should consist of stocks and longer-term bonds. But which stocks? And which bonds?

TIPS vs. Nominal Bonds

For the majority (or perhaps all) of the bond portion of the portfolio, I'd suggest using Treasury Inflation-Protected Securities (TIPS). TIPS are U.S. government bonds that provide a specific *after*-inflation return, in contrast to traditional "nominal" bonds that provide a specific before-inflation return. There are two primary reasons that I suggest TIPS for the bulk of your bond portfolio:

1. TIPS' inflation-adjusted yield makes them much more useful for planning purposes, and

2. In contrast to working-age investors, whose wages will typically keep up with inflation, retirees need a greater degree of protection from inflation risk.

Individual TIPS vs. TIPS Funds

When it comes to owning TIPS, you have two choices:

1. Buy them via a TIPS mutual fund or ETF, or
2. Buy them directly via a brokerage firm or via the U.S. Treasury's website at TreasuryDirect.gov.

The primary advantage of a TIPS fund is convenience. TIPS funds can be bought at any time, whereas individual TIPS are bought at auctions which only occur at specific intervals throughout the year. Similarly, you can sell a TIPS fund at any time (with no commission assuming it's a no-load fund), whereas selling individual TIPS generally involves paying a commission ($45 if your account is with Treasury Direct). Lastly, with a TIPS fund, you can have the interest reinvested automatically in the fund; with individual TIPS, you'll have to wait until the next auction date rolls around before you can reinvest the interest you've received.

Of course, buying individual TIPS has its own advantages. Firstly, you'll have lower expenses. Any TIPS fund will have to charge expenses. Yes, for good funds the expense ratio is quite low (multiple funds are available with expense ratios of 0.25% or less), but if you buy TIPS directly there will be no expenses eating into your returns. The second advantage of buying individual TIPS is that you know precisely what rate of return you'll get over the life of the bond. With a TIPS fund, you can't be as sure because the fund is made up of an always-changing collection of TIPS with varying maturities.

Stock Holdings: International vs. U.S.

The United States stock market makes up approximately 40% of the value of world stock markets.[1] Therefore, if you had no reason to prefer domestic stocks to international stocks (or vice versa), it would be reasonable to allocate approximately 40% of your portfolio to U.S. stocks.

As a retiree living in the U.S., however, you do have a reason to prefer U.S. stocks. That reason is known as "currency risk." Currency risk is the risk that your return from international stocks will be decreased as a result of the U.S. dollar increasing in value relative to the value of the currencies of the countries in which you have invested.

EXAMPLE: A portion of your portfolio is invested in Brazilian stocks, and over the next ten years those

---

[1] World markets as represented by the MSCI AC World Index.

stocks earn an annual return of 8%. However, over that same period, the Brazilian currency decreases in value relative to the dollar at a rate of 3% per year. When measured in U.S. dollars, your annual return would only be (approximately) 5%.

In other words, international stocks have an additional source of volatility: fluctuations in exchange rates. As we've discussed, volatility is *not a good thing* for a retirement portfolio. As such, it makes sense to use U.S. stocks for the bulk of your stock portfolio—perhaps somewhere between 70-80%. (Again, this is one of those things where we simply have no way to know the correct answer ahead of time.)

Putting it All Together

At the beginning of retirement, for an investor using a 4% starting withdrawal rate (such that one year of expenses = 4% of the portfolio), a low-cost index fund portfolio using the bucket method might look something like this:

- o   8% savings or money market account
- o   12% Vanguard Short-Term Treasury Index
- o   40% Vanguard Inflation-Protected Securities
- o   32% Vanguard Total Stock Market Index
- o   8% Vanguard Total International Stock Index[1]

Important note: This suggested asset allocation is based on a hypothetical investor, not based on your own personal circumstances. Your own risk tolerance, age at retirement, expected lifespan, ability to cut spending or return to work, and several other factors will play a role in determining *your own* appropriate allocation.

For example, if you're not comfortable with the unpredictability that comes with allocating such a large portion of your portfolio to stocks, that's OK. But if that's the case, you'll have to make appropriate adjustments, such as:

- o   Annuitizing a large portion of your portfolio via inflation-indexed single premium immediate annuities, or
- o   Sticking almost entirely with Treasury Inflation-Protected Securities and planning on a very low withdrawal rate from the beginning.

---

[1] The percentage allocation between cash and non-cash securities will naturally fluctuate over time depending on the performance of your stock and bond holdings.

Chapter 8 Simple Summary

- TIPS are ideal for the bond portion of a retirement portfolio because they protect against inflation, which can otherwise be a major risk for a retired investor.

- Buying TIPS directly will allow you to reduce your investment costs, but it's not as convenient as buying a TIPS index fund or ETF.

- In order to reduce currency risk, it's probably a good idea for a U.S. retiree to keep the majority of her stock holdings in U.S. stocks.

PART THREE

Tax Planning in Retirement

During retirement, the bulk of your income will come from your portfolio rather than from a job. As a result, the impact of tax planning for your portfolio becomes more apparent than it's ever been before: Every dollar of your investment returns that goes to taxes is a dollar that you don't get to spend.

As a quick refresher before we get started discussing tax planning strategies, the following page has a table comparing the three main categories of investment accounts. Please recognize, however, that:

o   There are exceptions to the information provided in the table, and
o   The table assumes that you've already met the various rules for taking IRA distributions without penalty.

Categories of Investment Accounts		
Type	**Examples**	**Tax Treatment**
Taxable	Taxable brokerage account	Interest is taxed at your ordinary income tax rate. Short-term capital gains are taxed at your ordinary income tax rate. Qualified dividends and long-term capital gains are taxed at a maximum rate of 15%. (And if you're in the 10% or 15% tax bracket, they're not taxed at all.)
Tax-deferred	Traditional IRA, 401(k), 403(b), 457(b)	Money contributed to the account (usually) reduces your taxable income in the year of the contribution. Money in the account is not taxed as it grows. Instead, when you take it out of the account, it's (usually) all taxable as ordinary income.
Tax-free	Roth IRA, Roth 401(k), Roth 403(b)	Money in the account is neither taxed as it grows, nor when you take it out of the account (because it was taxed before you put it in).

CHAPTER NINE

Roth Conversions

A Roth IRA conversion is a process through which you move money *from* a traditional IRA *to* a Roth IRA. The amount "converted" is taxable as income in the year of the conversion. In exchange, when you withdraw the money from your Roth, it comes out tax free.[1]

The typical motivation behind a Roth conversion is that it can lower your overall tax bill if you're in a lower tax bracket when you execute the conversion than you expect to be in later (when you take the money out of your Roth).

---

[1] If you take the money out prior to the first day of the fifth year after the date of the conversion, *and* you're under age 59½ when you take the distribution, it may be subject to a 10% penalty. See IRS Publication 590 for more details: www.irs.gov/publications/p590/
(Note: Pages on the IRS website will not load if you leave off the "www.")

Roth Conversion Eligibility

Prior to 2010, your income had to be under a certain level to be able to execute a Roth conversion. That's no longer the case. The income limits for Roth conversions are gone and are not scheduled to return.

In addition, rollovers to a Roth IRA are now permitted directly from a 401(k). Prior to 2008, you had to roll the 401(k) into a traditional IRA, then convert the traditional IRA to a Roth.

Lastly, the Small Business Jobs Act of 2010 permits participants in 401(k) and 403(b) plans to make *in-plan* Roth conversions in some cases. That is, you may be able to convert pre-tax 401(k) money to Roth 401(k) money without leaving the plan. Note, however, that this option is generally only available for amounts that would otherwise be eligible for a rollover and only if your plan allows Roth contributions.

But remember: Just because you *can* convert to a Roth doesn't mean you *should*. In most cases, a Roth conversion only makes sense if you expect to be in a higher tax bracket in the future than you're in at the moment. As you can imagine, this is not the case for most taxpayers immediately before retirement, as most taxpayers are in a *lower* tax bracket in retirement than they were in while they were working.

What Does This Have to Do With Retirement Planning?

Given the fact that eligibility for a Roth conversion has nothing to do with age or working status, you may wonder why I bring it up in a book on retirement planning. There are two reasons.

First, as we'll see in the next chapter, you have more control over your tax bracket from year to year during retirement than you do while you're working. This flexibility can give you more opportunities to benefit from a well-planned Roth conversion.

The second reason has to do with reaching age 59½. Specifically, prior to age 59½, it's generally unwise to execute a Roth conversion unless you have cash on hand to pay the tax on the conversion. If you use money from the IRA to pay the tax, that money will count as a distribution from your IRA. And, unless you meet one of a few exceptions[1], it will count as a "nonqualified distribution" from your IRA, and will be subject to a 10% penalty. Once you reach age 59½, distributions aren't subject to the 10% penalty, so the amount of cash you have on hand is no longer a concern.

EXAMPLE: Claire is 50 years old and married. She has decided that she wants to convert her entire $60,000 traditional IRA to a Roth IRA. Not count-

---

[1] You can find explanations of the potential exceptions in IRS Publication 590.

ing the conversion, her taxable income for the year is $70,000, putting her in the 25% tax bracket. Claire does not have any cash available with which to pay the tax on the conversion.

Claire takes all $60,000 out of her traditional IRA, moves $45,000 immediately into her Roth, and saves the remaining $15,000 in a taxable account to pay the (25%) income tax that will result from taking $60,000 out of her traditional IRA. Unfortunately, because she's not yet 59½, the $15,000 that does not make it into her Roth will count as a nonqualified distribution and will be subject to a 10% penalty.

EXAMPLE: Janice is 60 years old and married. Janice has decided that she wants to convert $40,000 from her traditional IRA to her Roth IRA. Not counting the conversion, Janice's taxable income for the year is $20,000, putting her in the 15% tax bracket. Like Claire, Janice doesn't have any cash on hand with which to pay the tax on the conversion.

Janice withdraws $40,000 from her traditional IRA, immediately moving $34,000 into her Roth. She saves the remaining $6,000 (15% of $40,000) in a taxable account to pay the tax on the conversion. Unlike Claire, Janice has reached age 59½, so the $6,000 that doesn't get converted will not count as a nonqualified distribution, and it will not be subject to the 10% penalty.

Takeaway: Once you're retired and you've reached age 59½, you have more flexibility to use Roth conversions for potential tax savings.

How to Execute a Roth Conversion

The best method for executing a Roth conversion is to do a direct transfer via your fund company or brokerage firm—either online or by calling them on the phone so they can walk you through the process.

You *can* do it yourself by withdrawing the funds from your traditional IRA, then depositing them in your Roth. But this exposes you to potential errors. Specifically, if everyday life distracts you, and you don't get the funds deposited into your Roth within 60 days, they'll no longer be eligible for conversion.

Roth Conversions of Non-Deductible Contributions

If your traditional IRA includes contributions that were not deductible when you made them (because your income was too high), a portion of your Roth conversion will not be taxable as income. The portion of the conversion that's not taxable is calculated as:

$$\text{Non-deductible contributions} \div \left(\begin{array}{c} \text{Traditional} \\ \text{IRA balance} \\ \textbf{as of 12/31} \end{array} + \begin{array}{c} \text{Distributions} \\ \text{\& conversions} \\ \text{made during} \\ \text{the year} \end{array} \right)$$

EXAMPLE: For the last 5 years, Lawrence has been making non-deductible contributions to his tradi-

tional IRA of $5,000 per year, for a total of $25,000. In June, Lawrence makes a $20,000 Roth conversion. At the end of the year, his traditional IRA is worth $55,000. One-third of his $20,000 conversion will be non-taxable, calculated as:
$25,000 ÷ ($55,000 + $20,000) = 0.33

Note: As we saw previously (page 43), the IRS considers all of your traditional IRA accounts to make up one traditional IRA. So even if Lawrence's IRA was split up among several IRA accounts at various brokerage firms, it would not change the calculation at all.

EXAMPLE (Part 2): Same example as above, except that Lawrence also rolls a $425,000 401(k) into his IRA in August. Lawrence's rollover changes the end-of-year value of his IRA, and, therefore, the portion of his conversion that is taxable.

Specifically, Lawrence's IRA is now worth $480,000 at the end of the year. As such, only 5% of his conversion will be non-taxable, calculated as:
$25,000 ÷ ($480,000 + $20,000) = 0.05.

Takeaway: If Lawrence wants to make a Roth conversion and roll over his 401(k), he may want to postpone the rollover until the year after the conversion has taken place, so as to minimize the portion of the conversion that's taxable.

Chapter 9 Simple Summary

- If you're currently in a lower tax bracket than you expect to be in later in retirement, you may be able to save money by converting your traditional IRA (or a portion of your traditional IRA) to a Roth IRA.

- While Roth conversions are helpful for any investor to understand, retirees (especially those over age 59½) have more flexibility to use them strategically.

- It's best to execute a Roth IRA conversion directly via your brokerage firm or fund company.

- If you have made non-deductible contributions to an IRA, a portion of your Roth conversion will be non-taxable.

CHAPTER TEN

Distribution Planning

The question of what type of retirement account to contribute to—Roth IRA, traditional IRA, 401(k), etc.—gets a lot of press. And that makes sense. If you choose correctly, you'll end up with a significantly higher after-tax balance when it comes time to spend your savings.

What doesn't get nearly as much press is how to minimize taxes by planning *distributions*[1] strategically. That is, should you take money out of your Roth IRA, traditional IRA, or taxable accounts first? Or should you be spending a little from each type of account every year?

Much like the question of which account to contribute to, the question of which account to withdraw from is largely a function of tax brackets—

---

[1] A withdrawal from a retirement account is referred to as a distribution.

and how you expect your future tax rate to compare to your current tax rate.

For the most part, it makes sense to follow a strategy along these lines:

1. Take distributions from tax-deferred accounts to fill up your 0% tax bracket.
2. Take distributions from tax-deferred accounts to fill up your 10% tax bracket, if you expect to be in a tax bracket greater than 10% later.
3. Repeat step #2 for each higher tax bracket—filling it up if you expect to be in a higher bracket later in retirement. (And, if you don't need to spend the money, converting it to a Roth IRA in most cases.)
4. If you still have spending needs to satisfy, spend first from taxable accounts, then from your Roth IRA.[1]

However, once you reach age 70 ½ and you have to start taking Required Minimum Distributions (RMDs), be sure to take them each year, regardless

---

[1] Potential exception: If you don't expect to spend your entire nest egg during your lifetime, it may make sense to spend from your Roth IRA before your taxable accounts in order to take advantage of the fact that your heirs would receive a "step up" in cost basis when they inherit your assets in taxable accounts. That is, when they inherit your assets, their cost basis will be the fair market value of the assets at the time of your death.

of the above strategy. The penalty on RMDs not taken by their deadline is steep enough that it outweighs other tax-saving considerations.

The following are the 2011 tax brackets for single taxpayers and married taxpayers filing jointly. They should be helpful as we go through a few examples.

Single (2011)

Taxable Income[1]:	The tax is:
$0 - $8,500	10% of the amount over $0
$8,500 - $34,500	$850 plus 15% of the amount over $8,500
$34,500 - $83,600	$4,750 plus 25% of the amount over $34,500
$83,600 - $174,400	$17,025 plus 28% of the amount over $83,600
$174,400 - $379,150	$42,449 plus 33% of the amount over $174,400
$379,151+	$110,016.50 plus 35% of the amount over $379,150

---

[1] Note: "Taxable income" refers to the amount that's left after subtracting all your deductions and exemptions from your total income.

Married Filing Jointly (2011)

Taxable Income:	The tax is:
$0 - $17,000	10% of the amount over $0
$17,000 - $69,000	$1,700 plus 15% of the amount over $17,000
$69,000 - $139,350	$9,500 plus 25% of the amount over $69,000
$139,350 - $212,300	$27,087.50 plus 28% of the amount over $139,350
$212,300 - $379,150	$47,513.50 plus 33% of the amount over $212,300
$379,151+	$102,574 plus 35% of the amount over $379,150

Fill the Bottom Tax Brackets

Based on the 2011 tax law, the first $19,000 of a married couple's income is not subject to Federal income tax at all (because of the $11,600 standard deduction and two exemptions of $3,700 each), and the next $17,000 is only taxed at a rate of 10%.

One way to minimize your overall tax burden is to take sufficient distributions from tax-deferred accounts to fill up the lowest tax brackets each year. It's preferable to pay 10% or 15% in taxes now rather than wait, take all the money out over the course of just a few years, and have the distributions bump you up into a higher tax bracket.

EXAMPLE: John and Janice are mostly retired. (John has started working part-time at a local garden-supply store.) John and Janice are both 60 years old, so they're not yet receiving Social Security. Between interest income and John's wages, they earn $15,000 over the course of the year. They need $28,000 to cover their living expenses. They could take the extra $13,000 out of a taxable account, Janice's Roth IRA, or John's traditional IRA.

Due to the standard deduction and personal exemptions, John and Janice's first $19,000 of income is free from income taxes. So it's clear that they should take at least $4,000 ($19,000 minus their $15,000 of other income) from their traditional IRA because it'll be entirely tax free.

After that, they'll still need to come up with another $9,000 to pay their bills. If John and Janice expect their marginal tax rate to be above 10% later in retirement (due to Social Security or required minimum distributions from their tax-deferred accounts, for instance), it would probably be a good idea for them to satisfy the rest of their income needs with distributions from the traditional IRA, thereby paying tax at 10% now rather than at a higher rate later. [Note: Because of the 10% tax, they'll have to take out $10,000 in order to have $9,000 left to pay bills.]

And by the same reasoning, it's likely a good idea to take an additional $7,000 distribution from their traditional IRA—even though they don't need to spend the money—in order to fill out the 10% tax bracket. [Because $7,000 is equal to $17,000 (the upper limit of the 10% bracket), minus $10,000 (the distribution they've already taken.)] They can then convert that money into a Roth IRA, thereby paying tax at their 10% rate now and avoiding tax at a higher rate later.

In fact, if John and Janice expect to have a marginal tax rate greater than 15% later in retirement, it may be a good idea for them to take another $52,000 out of their traditional IRA—thereby filling out their 15% tax bracket this year as well—and move it to a Roth IRA.[1] (More precisely, they'd want to move 85% of that amount to a Roth, saving the other 15% to pay tax on the distribution.)

Taxable Account before Roth

But what if you expect to be in approximately the same tax bracket all the way through retirement? In that case, after filling up your lowest bracket(s) with traditional IRA distributions, it's often best to spend from taxable accounts before spending from your Roth IRA. The reason for doing this is that Roth accounts are not taxed on their growth. As such, when choosing which account you'll allow to con-

---

[1] A taxpayer's "marginal tax rate" is the rate of tax that she would pay on her next dollar of income. For example, if a married couple has taxable income of $50,000 and their state charges a flat 3% tax rate, their total marginal tax rate would be 18% (15% Federal + 3% state).

tinue to grow, you're generally best served by choosing the one that can grow tax-free.

EXAMPLE: Constance is single, 70 years old, and retired. She has no intention of going back to work at any point. Her savings (spread equally between a traditional IRA, a Roth IRA, and a taxable account) are modest. So, barring changes in tax law, she doesn't expect to exceed the 10% tax bracket at any point in the future.

Tax-free Social Security income satisfies $12,000 of her $30,000 annual expenses. She also earns interest income of $2,000. So she still needs to satisfy $16,000 of expenses.

As a single taxpayer over age 65, her first $10,950 of income is free from income tax due to a $3,700 exemption and $7,250 standard deduction. So it makes sense for Constance to take at least $8,950 out of her traditional IRA because it will be taxed at a rate of 0% ($8,950 being $10,950, minus her $2,000 of interest income).[1]

Beyond that point, since Constance doesn't ever expect to be in a tax bracket higher than 10%, it doesn't make sense for her to take traditional IRA distributions at a 10% tax rate. Instead, her best plan is to satisfy her remaining expenses from her taxable

---

[1] This is somewhat of an oversimplification, as it assumes that Constance qualifies for no other deductions or credits whatsoever. If she does, she should take more out of her traditional IRA.

account, thereby maximizing the amount left to grow in her tax-advantaged accounts.

What about an investor who is early in retirement and expects to be in a lower tax bracket later? In that case, it's best to refrain from taking traditional IRA distributions. Instead, save the traditional IRA balance so that you can take distributions later, once you're in that lower tax bracket. In the meantime, spend first from taxable accounts, then from a Roth IRA if necessary.

EXAMPLE: Raymond and Louisa are 60 years old. Raymond is retired, but Louisa doesn't plan to retire for a few more years. Louisa earns $37,000 this year, which is just shy of their $39,000 annual living expenses.

Louisa's income puts them in the 15% tax bracket. Once Louisa retires, they expect to be in the 10% tax bracket. As a result, it doesn't make sense to fund their remaining expenses with traditional IRA distributions (paying tax at a 15% rate) when they could wait and pay tax at a 10% rate later. Louisa and Raymond decide, therefore, to use some of their taxable holdings to fund their remaining expenses this year (thereby also allowing their Roth to continue its tax-free growth for as long as possible).

Social Security: It's Complicated.

Once an investor begins receiving Social Security benefits, things become even more complicated.

The complicating factor is that, as your income proceeds through the 15% bracket, the portion of your Social Security income that is subject to income tax increases as well. In effect, this leads to a segment of the 15% tax bracket in which your marginal tax rate is actually *higher* than 15% (because each additional dollar of income is not only taxed at 15%, but also increases the amount of social security that is taxable).

The same general process as described on page 70 still applies: Take distributions from your traditional IRA if you're currently in a lower tax bracket than you expect to be in later. Then spend from your taxable account, then from your Roth IRA. The only thing that changes is that the questions "what tax bracket am I in" and "what tax bracket will I be in later" become significantly more complicated.[1]

As you might imagine, a financial planner with expertise in tax planning and Social Security benefits can be very helpful here. Spending a few hundred dollars to sit down with such a professional

---

[1] For a thorough discussion of taxation of social security benefits, see IRS Publication 915, available at: www.irs.gov/publications/p915/

could quite possibly save you several thousand dollars in taxes.

Chapter 10 Simple Summary

- Strategically planning which accounts to spend from first can reduce your overall tax burden throughout retirement.

- In general, it makes sense to take traditional IRA distributions up to the point at which further distributions would put you into a tax bracket that is higher than the tax bracket you expect to be in later in retirement. (Note: If you expect a *lower* tax bracket later in retirement, this amount will be zero.)

- If, after taking such traditional IRA distributions, you still need to liquidate other investments, it's usually best to spend from your taxable account prior to spending from your Roth IRA.

- A financial planner who is knowledgeable about tax planning and Social Security planning has the potential to save you a great deal of money.

CHAPTER ELEVEN

Asset Location

Asset location is the process of determining which investments to keep in which accounts. That is, after you've determined your appropriate asset allocation, how should you divvy up your investments between tax-sheltered accounts and taxable accounts?

EXAMPLE: Terry is 65 years old and retired. He has decided that his appropriate asset allocation is a simple 40/60 stock/bond split. He currently has $275,000 in a traditional IRA, $75,000 in a Roth IRA, and another $150,000 invested in taxable accounts.

So, Terry's grand total portfolio is $500,000, and he would like $200,000 (40%) invested in stocks and $300,000 (60%) invested in bonds.

How should Terry go about divvying up each of his accounts between stocks and bonds? The following table outlines four possible options:

	Tax-Sheltered Accounts		Taxable Account
	Traditional IRA	**Roth IRA**	**Account**
1	$165,000 bonds $110,000 stocks	$45,000 bonds $30,000 stocks	$90,000 bonds $60,000 stocks
2	$275,000 bonds	$25,000 bonds $50,000 stocks	$150,000 stocks
3	$150,000 bonds $125,000 stocks	$75,000 stocks	$150,000 bonds
4	$100,000 bonds $175,000 stocks	$75,000 bonds	$125,000 bonds $25,000 stocks

Most investors wouldn't put a lot of thought into the difference between the above scenarios. After all, each of them results in a portfolio that has $300,000 of bonds and $200,000 of stocks. But, as we'll see in a minute, Terry can save some money on taxes by choosing option #2 because it's the scenario in which all of his bonds are in tax-sheltered accounts.

Tax-Shelter Your Bonds

From a tax standpoint, it's beneficial to tax-shelter your bonds (that is, put them in an IRA of some sort) before tax-sheltering your stocks. Why? Because stocks are already more tax-efficient than bonds.

Bond interest is taxed as ordinary income, at whatever your marginal tax rate happens to be. In contrast, stock gains come in the form of either dividends (which, for the moment, are usually taxed at a maximum rate of 15%) or capital gains (which, if the holding period for the stock was greater than one year, are also taxed at a maximum rate of 15%). As a result, you stand to benefit more from tax-sheltering your bonds than you do from tax-sheltering your stocks.

In addition to their favorable tax rates, stocks are more tax-efficient than bonds for the following reasons:

- o Because they're more volatile, stocks will provide more opportunities for tax-loss harvesting,[1]
- o Foreign stock holdings are often eligible for the foreign tax credit (which we'll cover momentarily), and
- o Because capital gains are not taxed until the investment is sold, stocks are already tax-deferred to some extent.

---

[1] For a more thorough discussion of tax-loss harvesting, see: bogleheads.org/wiki/Tax_Loss_Harvesting

Tax-Shelter Your REITs

As is common with topics involving taxation, there's an exception to the general guideline of tax-sheltering bonds before stocks. Specifically, if you own any Real Estate Investment Trusts (REITs) or REIT funds, you'll likely want to make it a priority to tax-shelter them, even though they're stocks. The reason is that REITs' dividends are *not* considered to be "qualified dividends," so they're taxed as ordinary income. In addition, REITs' payoff comes primarily in the form of these non-qualified dividends, rather than capital gains. As a result, REITs are very tax-inefficient and should be tax-sheltered if at all possible.

Tax-Shelter Your TIPS

Treasury Inflation-Protected Securities (TIPS) provide protection from inflation because their principal value is adjusted in keeping with inflation. (The interest payments, which are based on the inflation-adjusted principal, are therefore adjusted for inflation as well.)

These adjustments to the principal value of the bond are taxable as income in the year they occur, even though the owner of the TIPS doesn't actually receive the increased principal value until the bond matures. As a result, TIPS are somewhat less efficient from a cash-flow standpoint than most other bonds when held in a taxable account. Therefore, it's usually best to tax-shelter them before tax-sheltering your other fixed-income investments.

Foreign Tax Credit

After tax-sheltering your REITs and your bonds, if you have a choice between tax-sheltering your domestic stocks or your international stocks, it's generally best to tax-shelter your domestic holdings, so as to take advantage of the foreign tax credit.

What's the foreign tax credit? The IRS explains it this way: "You can claim a credit for foreign taxes that are imposed on you by a foreign country or U.S. possession." In other words, the idea of the credit is to eliminate double taxation on foreign income.

EXAMPLE: In your taxable brokerage account, you earn $1,000 of dividend income over the course of the year from your non-U.S. stocks, and you pay $100 in foreign taxes on that income. You can claim a $100 credit for foreign taxes paid, thereby reducing your U.S. income tax obligation by $100.

It's important to note that investments held in a retirement account—like an IRA or 401(k)—do not qualify for the credit. This is why, when making asset location decisions, it's best to tax-shelter your domestic stock funds before tax-sheltering your international stock funds.

Foreign Tax Credit and Mutual Funds

According to IRS Publication 514, "If you are a shareholder of a mutual fund...you may be able to claim the credit based on your share of foreign income taxes paid by the fund if it chooses to pass the credit on to its shareholders."

The tricky part here is that funds that own other mutual funds (target retirement date funds, for instance) don't qualify. Why? Because *they* don't pay the foreign taxes—the underlying funds pay them. So if you're looking for an international stock fund to hold in a taxable account, it's worth paying attention to whether or not the fund qualifies for the foreign tax credit.

Tax-Sheltering Priority List

In summary, the typical priority for tax-sheltering investments is as follows:

1. REITS
2. TIPS
3. Other fixed income
4. Domestic stocks
5. International stocks

Remember: With very few exceptions[1], even the most tax-efficient investments are better off in a tax-sheltered account than in a taxable account. So if you have sufficient room in your retirement accounts to tax-shelter everything, it's generally wise to do so.

Chapter 11 Simple Summary

- Stocks are generally more tax-efficient than bonds. As a result, it's usually best to tax-shelter your bonds before your stocks.

- Because of the foreign tax credit, international stocks are generally more tax-efficient than domestic stocks. As a result, it's usually best to tax-shelter domestic stocks first.

- REITs and TIPS are both decidedly tax-inefficient. As such, they're the highest priority for tax-sheltering.

---

[1] Most notably, municipal bonds, which pay interest that's free from Federal income tax.

CHAPTER TWELVE

Other Tips for Taxable Accounts

Whether due to downsizing on living space, selling a business, or having socked away more money per year than you could contribute to retirement accounts, it's likely that at retirement age, you have more assets in taxable accounts than you've had (or will have) at any other time in your life.

My suggestions for investing in taxable accounts can be summed up as follows:

1. Make intelligent asset location decisions, and
2. Choose tax-efficient investments whenever possible.

We covered asset location in the previous chapter, so let's take a look at how to select tax-efficient investments.

Look for Low Portfolio Turnover

A mutual fund's "portfolio turnover" refers to the portion of the assets held by the fund that were bought or sold over the course of the year. Higher turnover always leads to higher costs in terms of commissions and bid/ask spreads. And, if you're investing in a taxable account, higher turnover leads to higher taxes as well.

The reason that high portfolio turnover leads to higher taxes is that the fund's capital gains distributions will be primarily short-term rather than long-term, and they will therefore be taxed at your ordinary income tax rate rather than the more favorable long-term capital gains tax rate. Higher turnover also minimizes the potential for delaying taxes on capital appreciation.

For the most part, index funds and ETFs have low portfolio turnover and are, therefore, fairly tax-efficient (relative to otherwise-comparable actively managed funds at least). That said, there are some other choices that can be even more tax-friendly.

"Tax-Managed" Funds

One tax-efficient alternative to index funds is to use "tax-managed" mutual funds—funds that are specifically managed to minimize distributions of capital gains.

For example, Vanguard offers five low-cost, tax-managed funds. (In fact, the funds have lower expense ratios than the comparable index funds.) The drawbacks are that they have a $10,000 minimum investment, and they carry a 1% redemption fee if the fund is sold within 5 years. This redemption fee can potentially get in the way of rebalancing and tax-loss harvesting.[1]

To get an idea of the potential savings from using a given tax-managed fund, I'd suggest finding the fund (and the non-tax-managed alternative) on Morningstar's website. Under the "tax" heading, you'll see the fund's "tax cost ratio," which gives an estimate of how large a bite taxes would have taken out of the fund's return for an investor in the highest tax bracket. [2] (The higher your tax bracket, the more you stand to gain from using tax-managed funds.)

Tax-Exempt Bonds

As we discussed in the previous chapter, it's generally best to tax-shelter your bonds if possible. But if you have to own bond funds in a taxable account,

---

[1] One of the funds, Vanguard Tax-Managed International, has an ETF share class (ticker: VEA), which would allow you to get around the redemption fee and minimum investment.

[2] By way of example: For the decade ending 8/31/2010, Morningstar estimates a tax cost ratio of 0.62% annually for an investor in Vanguard Small Cap Index, and a tax cost ratio of just 0.17% per year for an investor in Vanguard Tax-Managed Small-Cap.

you should consider using tax-exempt municipal bonds.[1] To determine whether it's advantageous to use tax-exempt bonds, compare their yield to the after-tax yield that you could get on a taxable bond fund of similar credit rating.

EXAMPLE: As of this writing, the yield on Vanguard's Total Bond Market Index Fund was 2.41%. If you're in the 28% tax bracket, this would provide an after-tax yield of 1.74%, calculated as 2.41% x 0.72. This tells you that, if a tax-exempt bond fund of similar credit rating and maturity is yielding greater than 1.74%, the tax-exempt fund would be a good choice.

Note: If your state exempts its own municipal bonds from state income tax and you have access to a low-cost bond fund that invests exclusively in tax-exempt bonds from within your state, be sure to use your combined state and Federal tax rate when determining after-tax yield.

EXAMPLE: If you live in New Jersey and are in the 28% Federal tax bracket and 6.37% state tax bracket (for a total tax rate of 34.37%), your after-tax yield on Vanguard's Total Bond Market Index Fund as of this writing would be 1.58%, calculated as 2.41% x 0.6563. As such, if you can find a low-cost fund of

---

[1] Bonds issued by states and municipalities are free from Federal income tax.

tax-exempt New Jersey municipal bonds yielding greater than 1.58%, it may be a better choice.

If you're considering investing in municipal bonds, remember that they carry credit risk (that is, the risk that the bond issuer will default on the debt). This means that:

1. It's important to diversify among issuers. (Investing via a fund makes this easier.)
2. For it to make sense to invest in municipal bonds, they must offer a higher after-tax yield than Treasury bonds of a similar maturity. Otherwise there's no reason to take on the additional risk.

Avoid Funds of Funds

Balanced funds and target date funds can be an excellent, hands-off way to implement an asset allocation strategy. Owning such funds in a taxable account, however, is generally not a good idea for a handful of reasons.

First, as we discussed in the previous chapter, balanced funds and target date funds are often "funds of funds", which makes them unqualified for the foreign tax credit.

Second, the bond portion of such funds' portfolios are typically made up of taxable bonds (or taxable bond funds). This isn't inherently bad, but if you're in one of the top tax brackets, you may be better off with tax-exempt bonds.

Third, because they include both stocks and bonds in a single fund, they get in the way of an asset location strategy. If you have assets in both taxable accounts and tax-sheltered accounts, it's best to own your bond funds and stock funds separately so that you can place them in the most advantageous accounts.

Finally, in their efforts to maintain a constant asset allocation, balanced funds and target date funds often rebalance extremely frequently, leading to high portfolio turnover.

Realizing Capital Gains

One final note about investing in taxable accounts: If you have a large unrealized capital gain built up in a tax-inefficient investment, it may not make sense to sell that investment in order to move your money into something more tax-efficient. You'll have to weigh the cost of paying tax on the gain now against the savings you hope to gain in the future with a more tax-efficient alternative.

Chapter 12 Simple Summary

- The lower a fund's portfolio turnover, the more tax-efficient it's likely to be.

- Tax-managed mutual funds are designed specifically to minimize the impact of income taxes on the fund's investors. The higher your tax bracket, the more potentially advantageous this can be.

- Depending on your tax bracket and current interest rates, tax-exempt municipal bonds may offer a higher after-tax yield than taxable bonds with similar credit risk and maturity. Remember, though, that they carry more credit risk than Treasury bonds, so it's important to diversify among issuers.

- "Funds of funds" (such as balanced funds or target date funds) are generally tax-inefficient for several reasons. It's often wise to avoid them when investing in a taxable account.

CONCLUSION

Getting Help with Your Plan

In my book *Investing Made Simple*, I wrote that most investors do not need a financial advisor if they're willing to take the time to learn all the ins and outs of managing a portfolio. I still believe that to be the case.

I also wrote, however, that as an investor gets closer to retirement, the usefulness of an advisor increases dramatically. By the time you retire, your portfolio is (hopefully) quite substantial in size. Therefore, mistakes are more costly than they've ever been. And at age 60, you have fewer remaining working years to make up for mistakes than you had at age 30.

In addition, as we've seen throughout this book, the complexity involved with a retirement-stage portfolio is far greater than that of an accumulation-stage portfolio. Whoever is managing your finances (whether you or an advisor), is going to have to:

1. Create a portfolio that will a) provide sufficient income to satisfy your needs over a multiple-decade retirement, b) keep up with inflation, c) minimize the return-damaging effects of volatility, and d) account for sequence of returns risk,
2. Determine the most advantageous order of distributions from your various accounts,
3. Determine how Roth conversions fit into that distribution plan,
4. Develop an asset location plan that will minimize your taxes while still providing sufficient liquidity, and
5. Adjust all of the above as necessary to account for changes in your life or changes in tax law.

While I believe that a motivated individual with sufficient free time and math skills can certainly get the job done on his or her own, many retirees stand to benefit from a meeting (or, more likely, ongoing meetings) with an advisor.

Important Areas of Expertise

As you can see from the list above, if you decide to use the services of an advisor, you'll want to look for somebody who can do more than just set up a portfolio. You want an advisor who is truly an expert in retirement planning. Among other things, this person should be knowledgeable about:

- o IRA distribution planning,
- o Social Security strategies,
- o The interaction between Social Security and income tax and the tax-planning opportunities that interaction creates,
- o Using asset allocation to control risk,
- o Using asset location to minimize taxes, and
- o Using annuities to offset longevity risk and what to look for (or avoid) in an annuity.

Certain certifications can be helpful indicators of expertise. For example, somebody who is a Certified Financial Planner (CFP) is going to be knowledgeable about both taxation and investing. Alternatively, a CPA with the PFS (Personal Financial Specialist) designation is likewise going to be an expert on both taxation and investment planning.

You can find a CFP near you by visiting www.cfp.net/search/. You can find a local CPA with the PFS designation by visiting www.findapfs.org. (Note: This site doesn't load if you omit the www.)

Investment Philosophy

As we discussed briefly in Chapter 5, most mutual fund managers fail to outperform their respective indexes. And these people are intelligent, full-time professionals.

You should, therefore, be wary of any financial advisor who suggests that he can reliably earn above-market returns. After all, in addition to running your portfolio and the portfolios of all his other clients, this person has to perform marketing services for his business, keep up with tax law changes, stay up to date with regulatory and compliance issues, and much more. To think that—in his remaining time—he can achieve something that most full-time professionals fail to achieve is unreasonably optimistic.

Advisor Compensation

Finally, after narrowing your options down to advisors with sufficient expertise and realistic investment philosophies, you'll want to be careful to choose an advisor with a compensation structure that's a good fit for your needs. In most cases, the goal is to eliminate as many conflicts of interest as possible while still being affordable.

Commission-Paid Advisors

In short, I'd suggest staying away from advisors who use commission as a compensation structure. It creates too many conflicts of interest.

For example, if you use ETFs or individual stocks, a commission-paid advisor will have an incentive to convince you to move your money around more often than is beneficial, in order to collect a commission on each trade.

If you prefer mutual funds, a commission-paid advisor is only going to be able to recommend funds that charge a commission (known as a sales load). This is unfortunate, because these funds are usually actively managed funds with annual operating costs several times what you'd pay with a low-cost index fund.

"Assets Under Management" Advisors

Many people claim that the best advisor is one who is paid as a function of your account size (i.e., your "assets under management" or "AUM"). AUM fees tie the advisor's interests to yours...or so goes the claim. What they really do is tie the advisor's interests to your *account size*, not to your overall financial wellbeing.

EXAMPLE: Dennis is 70-years old. He has a $500,000 portfolio, from which he needs to withdraw $30,000 each year. In other words, Dennis is looking at a 6.00% withdrawal rate–higher than many people would consider safe, even for a 70-year-old.

 In such a scenario, a single premium immediate annuity might make a lot of sense. If Dennis buys single premium immediate annuities with, say, $400,000 of his portfolio, he could (as of this writing) get a payout of 6.2%, thereby leaving him with a safer withdrawal rate of 5.2% on the rest of his portfolio.[1]

---

[1] I use $400,000 here simply because it's a nice round number. For a more thorough discussion of how to

But if Dennis is currently using an advisor who charges based on account size—let's say 0.5% of assets—the advisor stands to gain *$2,000 each year* (0.5% times $400,000) by convincing Dennis *not* to buy the annuity.

Please understand that I'm not saying that advisors who charge commissions or assets under management-based fees are crooks who give the advice that's most profitable to them. As you can imagine, that's not the case at all. Most financial advisors are good people who seek to put their clients' interests first. Still, even for ethical, honest advisors, it can be difficult to see the merit of a particular strategy if their income benefits from not seeing such merit.

Hourly or Fee-for-Service Advisors

Other advisors charge based on a simple hourly fee or a fee-for-service arrangement in which you pay a flat fee for a given service (e.g., $X for an annual portfolio checkup). Like the other methods of advisor compensation, this one suffers from its own conflicts of interest. Hourly advisors need to keep you coming back year after year, so they don't have much incentive to teach you to manage your portfolio on your own (which could be a problem if that's your eventual goal). They also have somewhat of an

---

calculate how much of your portfolio to annuitize, please refer back to page 23.

incentive to over-plan—that is, to do more analysis on any given question than is really necessary.

That said, if I had to suggest one compensation structure, this is the one I would suggest, as I think it does the best job of eliminating conflicts of interest.

Take Your Time

As you might imagine, it can take time to find an advisor who has the expertise you need, an investment philosophy you believe in, and a compensation structure that minimizes conflicts of interest while still being affordable. That's OK. This is not a decision you want to rush.

My parting message for do-it-yourself investors is similar: The decisions you make with your portfolio immediately before and after retirement will have a dramatic impact on your standard of living going forward. So remember: There's no need to rush. With each decision, take your time and educate yourself fully before making any major changes.

And on that note, I'll leave you with my suggestions for further reading.

Appendix:
Suggestions for Further Reading

The Bogleheads' Guide to Retirement Planning, by Taylor Larimore, Mel Lindauer, Richard Ferri, Laura Dogu, and more

Common Sense on Mutual Funds: Fully Updated 10th Anniversary Edition, by John C. Bogle

Explore TIPS: A Practical Guide to Investing in Treasury Inflation-Protected Securities, by The Finance Buff

The Investor's Manifesto, by William J. Bernstein

The Little Book of Safe Money: How to Conquer Killer Markets, Con Artists, and Yourself, by Jason Zweig

The New Coffeehouse Investor, by Bill Schultheis

The Only Guide You'll Ever Need to the Right Financial Plan, by Larry Swedroe

A Random Walk Down Wall Street, by Burton G. Malkiel

Unveiling the Retirement Myth, by Jim Otar

Acknowledgements

As always, my thanks go to my editing team: Michelle, Pat, Debbi, and Kalinda. Once again, you've impressed me with your ability to make my writing readable.

Also, my sincere gratitude goes to the following people who were kind enough to contribute their time and expertise to help catch my errors and omissions: Dylan Ross, CFP; Jim Blankenship, CFP, EA; Thomas Booker, CPA; and Taylor Larimore, esteemed Boglehead author.

Finally, thanks to you, the reader. It's a dream come true to get to do this for a living.

A Note on IRS Publications

Throughout the book, I reference a few IRS Publications, as I believe that they're a helpful source of information for most taxpayers. Please note, however, that IRS Publications do not count as legal authority.

Notes on Data

Bond returns are calculated as the total return on 10-year U.S. Treasury Bonds, using data from the Federal Reserve Bank of St. Louis. This data can be found at: http://research.stlouisfed.org/

Stock market returns are calculated as the total return on the S&P 500 index. While this data can be found in many places, one excellent source is the 2010 Ibbotson SBBI Classic Yearbook. ("SBBI" stands for "Stocks, bonds, bills, and inflation.")

About the Author:

Mike is the author of seven personal finance books as well as the popular blog ObliviousInvestor.com.

Also by Mike Piper:

Accounting Made Simple: Accounting Explained in 100 Pages or Less

Investing Made Simple: Investing in Index Funds Explained in 100 Pages or Less

Oblivious Investing: Building Wealth by Ignoring the Noise

Surprisingly Simple: Independent Contractor, Sole Proprietor, and LLC Taxes Explained in 100 Pages or Less

Surprisingly Simple: LLC vs. S-Corp vs. C-Corp Explained in 100 Pages or Less

Taxes Made Simple: Income Taxes Explained in 100 Pages or Less

INDEX